LIFEWATCH

The Mystery of Nature

Acorn to Oak Tree

Oliver S. Owen

Published by Abdo & Daughters, 4940 Viking Drive, Suite 622, Edina, Minnesota 55435.

Library bound edition distributed by Rockbottom Books, Pentagon Tower, P.O. Box 36036, Minneapolis, Minnesota 55435.

Printed in the United States.

Cover Photo credit: Peter Arnold
Interior Photo credits: Stock Market— pages 7, 18, 24, 25, 27
Peter Arnold— pages 4, 6, 8, 9, 10, 13, 21, 25
Earth Scenes— pages 22, 23

Edited By: Bob Italia

LIBRARY OF CONGRESS CATALOGING-IN-PUBLICATION DATA

Owen, Oliver S., 1920—
    Acorn to Oak Tree / Oliver S. Owen.
        p.   cm. -- (Life Watch)
    Includes Bibliographical references (p.29) Glossary (p. 28) Index (p. 30).
    ISBN 1-56239-289-1
    1. Oak -- Life cycles -- Juvenile literature. 2. Acorns -- Juvenile literature.
    [1. Oak. 2. Trees. 3. Acorns.] I. Title. II. Series.
    QK495.F14094   1994
    583'.976--dc20   94-6302
                                            CIP
                                            AC

Contents

The Mighty Oak Tree

The Oak Tree

Take a good look at this oak. It is a mighty tree. It grows tall. It lives a long time. The bark is grayish-brown. Suppose you rubbed your hand over the bark. You would find it very rough. It has many ridges and grooves. The oak tree needs its bark. Without it, the tree would die. Look at the trunk. It holds the branches and leaves in the air. Look at the branches. See how crooked they are. That's a good way to tell that this is an oak tree. Look at the leaves. They flutter in the breeze. They are often bathed in sunlight.

What color are they? In autumn they become golden or reddish-brown. Soon they fall off the tree. One part of the tree you cannot see. The roots! They grow deep in the ground. They branch and rebranch many times. Look closely at the tree again. Do you see the acorns? There may be more than a thousand on one tree.

This is an oak tree in the autumn. See how the leaves turn colors.

Many kinds of animals make homes in oak trees. Squirrels and birds nest in the branches. Raccoons, woodpeckers and owls raise families in the hollows of dead oaks.

This squirrel has made his home in this oak tree. Oak trees have many cracks and holes that make good shelters for animals.

The Acorn

Big oaks may grow from tiny acorns. The acorn is a special kind of nut. One end is rounded. The other end fits into a cup. The acorns start forming in spring. They get bigger and bigger. By summer they are full size and green. They ripen by autumn and turn brown. Then they fall to the ground. Inside the acorn is a "baby oak." The part of the acorn around the "baby oak" is stored food. It is rich in energy. The "baby oak" will use this food to grow.

These two acorns are different ages. The brown acorn sprouted in the spring and the green acorn sprouted in the summer. Both will eventually fall in the autumn.

Spring acorn

Summer acorn

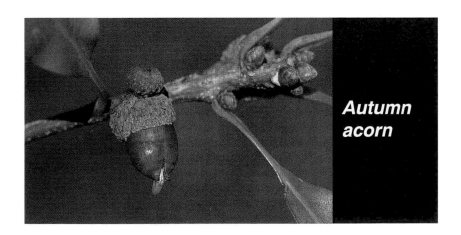

Autumn acorn

The Fallen Acorn

Some acorns don't fall to the ground. They may fall on the street, the roof of your house, or on your school playground. They may even hit you on the head while you walk to school! But most acorns drop from the oak to the ground. Not all acorns will grow into oaks. Maybe only one in a thousand. What happens to the others? They may die because of drought. Rainfall may wash them into a stream. They may be crushed by cattle or deer walking through the woods. They may be eaten by animals. Squirrels, raccoons, turkeys and grouse find them very "tasty." So do blue jays.

Suppose that a blue jay wants to store some acorns. The jay will pick one up with its bill. Then it will fly away with

Acorns are among the squirrel's favorite foods.

the acorn. It might fly as far as a mile or more. The jay will then bury the acorn in the ground. The jay stores the acorn so it doesn't go hungry when food is hard to find. But suppose it forgets where it buried the acorn. Then the acorn has a chance to grow into a mighty oak! Oak trees can thank the blue jays. Without them, there would be fewer oaks.

This photo shows a blue jay with an acorn in its mouth.

The Sprouting Acorn

The acorn lies in the ground a long time. Winter comes. It gets very cold. A fluffy blanket of snow covers the acorn. But the "baby oak" inside the acorn stays alive. Then spring comes. It gets warmer. The snow melts. And the oak embryo begins to grow! It soaks up water from melting snow. It gets energy from the food stored in the acorn. It sends down a tiny root. The root breaks through the acorn's shell. It grows into the soil. The "baby oak" is thirsty and hungry. The tiny root draws water from the soil. This helps the "baby oak" grow. A tiny shoot grows upward from the acorn. It forms little leaves. The leaves are bathed with sunlight. Then they turn green and can make sugar. The sugar is rich in energy. The "baby oak" uses this energy to grow. It also uses it to make leaves, roots, and a stem. The stem will become the tree trunk.

The tiny acorn is the beginning of the mighty oak tree.

The Oak Seedling

The young oak is called a seedling. It grows much slower than most trees. On its first "birthday" it may be only a few inches high. Not many seedlings live. They may be eaten by animals. They may be killed by disease. They may dry up if there is no rain.

This is the seedling of a Red Oak Tree.

These are the leaves of a Red Oak Seedling.

The Oak Sapling

By the time the seedlings are about ten years old they may be six feet tall. They are then called saplings. Look at the sapling's photo. See the grayish-brown bark? The oak is called a sapling until its trunk is about four inches thick. A sapling often has very large leaves. One sapling might have several hundred leaves. They make sugar for the growing oak. But they can do this only in sunlight. With enough water and sunshine, the sapling will grow taller. Its trunk will get thicker. When the trunk is more than four inches thick the sapling has "grown up" into a young oak.

This is a forest full of young oak saplings.

The Mighty Oak Tree
The Trunk

How long can you expect to live? The average person lives about 75 years. Oaks can do much better. Some oaks in England are more than 900 years old! How do we know the trees' age? Their trunks count their age. Have you ever looked at a tree stump? Did you see the "rings"? Each year the oak makes one of these "age rings." Suppose you come across an oak stump in the forest that has 20 "age rings." Then you would know that the oak is 20 years old.

The trunk of an oak tree has rings which identify its age.

Oak trees get very big. Have you ever tried to "hug" a tree? You couldn't get your arms around the big oaks. Some have trunks that are more than eight feet thick. A tunnel could be cut through the trunk big enough for your family car. The oak's trunk is its "skeleton." It holds up the oak's body. How much do you weigh? Sixty pounds? Your skeleton holds your 60-pound body four feet in the air. But the trunk "skeletons" of some oaks have much bigger jobs. They hold 5,000-pound trees 80 feet in the air.

The mighty oak is a very large tree. In this photo you can see how thick this oak is compared to the girl standing next to it.

The Bark

The trunk is more than a skeleton. It has another big job. On a hot summer day, oaks get very thirsty. They need a lot of water. So then the "pipes" in the trunk go to work. They carry water to the dry branches and leaves. More than 1,000 gallons might move through the "pipes" in a single day.

Look at the bark of the full-grown oak. Rub your hands over the bark. You'll find it very rough. The bark has many ridges and grooves. Without the bark the oak would die. What does it do for the oak? It holds water in the tree. It protects the tree from beetles that like to eat wood. It protects the oak from deer that "polish" their sharp antlers on tree trunks. And it protects the oak from disease and decay.

The bark of the oak tree moves water and nutrients throughout the tree. It also protects the tree from beetles that eat wood.

The Roots

Let's look at the roots. On a full-grown oak, they grow deep into the ground. They can split rocks. They can make sidewalks bulge and crack. They do a lot of work for the tree. They anchor it to the ground. Even if the wind blows 70 miles an hour, the oak won't fall. The oak's roots may have more than a trillion branches. You can only see the smallest ones with a microscope. Suppose we laid one tree's roots end-to-end. The line of roots would reach half way around the Earth at the equator!

The oak tree has a massive root system. In this photo you can see the beginnings of the root system at the base of this oak tree.

The powerful oak tree often grows up through hard surfaces like rock or even cement sidewalks.

The Leaves

A full-grown oak has more than one million leaves. In autumn they drop to the ground. Then the oak looks pretty bare. But it gets a new set of leaves the following spring. An oak tree cannot live long without its leaves. They are the tree's "food factories." They make energy-rich sugar. The tree uses this energy to grow tall, and to make new leaves, flowers and acorns. The leaves also release oxygen into the air. So do other green plants. That's good for all creatures. We breathe this oxygen into our lungs. Without oxygen humans and animals could not survive. The full-grown oak is a beautiful tree.

The beginning of an oak leaf is called a blossom.

Frost on the leaves of a white oak.

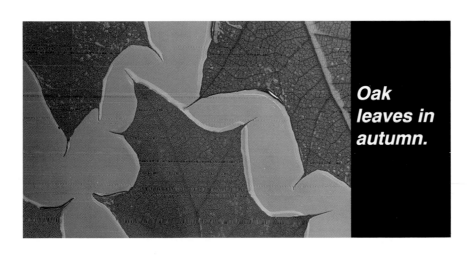

Oak leaves in autumn.

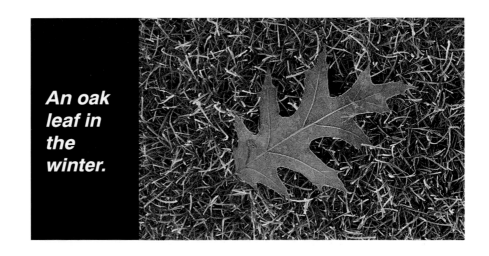

An oak leaf in the winter.

Years ago the American poet Joyce Kilmer wrote a simple little poem. It is one of the most-loved poems in America. It is called *Trees*. Here are a few lines:

> "I think that I shall never see
> a poem lovely as a tree,
> poems are made by fools like me,
> but only God can make a tree!"

And, of course, the oak is one of the mightiest and most beautiful of them all. That tiny acorn, about the size of your thumbnail, did a pretty good job!

The oak tree is one of the strongest and most beautiful trees in nature.

Glossary

Acorn   a special kind of nut made by an oak tree which contains the "baby oak" and a supply of stored food.

Bark   the tough, hard outer covering of a tree which protects the tree from water loss, insects and disease.

Drought   a period of dryness.

Embryo   the "baby oak" inside the acorn.

Leaves   blade-like parts which grow from branches; they make energy-rich food for the tree.

Oxygen   life-giving gas released from the green leaves of the oak tree.

Root   underground parts of the tree which take in water and food from the soil as well as anchor the tree.

Sapling   a young oak tree which has a trunk less than four inches thick.

Bibliography

Elias, Thomas S. *Trees of North America*. New York: Van Nostrand
    Reinhold, 1980.

Little, Elbert L. *The Audubon Society Field Guide to North American
    Trees*. New York: Alfred A. Knopf, 1987.

Scott, Jane. *Botany in the Field*. Englewood Cliffs, New Jersey:
    Prentice Hall, 1984.

Wiggers, Raymond. *Tree Leaves*. New York: Franklin Watts, 1991.

Index

About the Author

Oliver S. Owen is a Professor Emeritus for the University of Wisconsin at Eau Claire. He is the coauthor of *Natural Resource Conservation: An Ecological Approach* (Macmillan, 1991). Dr. Owen has also authored *Eco-Solutions* and *Intro to Your Environment* (Abdo & Daughters, 1993). Dr. Owen has a Ph.D. in zoology from Cornell University.

To my grandson, Amati,
may you grow up to always
appreciate and love nature.
— Grandpa Ollie